ENGLISH SPANISH DICTIONARY BY TOPICS

West Publishing

Table of Contents

Pronouns	los pronombres	7
Basic phrases	Frases clave	7
How to address a person	Cómo dirigirse a una persona	8
Numbers from 0 to 100	Números de 0 a 100	8
Numbers from 100 to milliard	Números de 100 a mil millones	9
Ordinal Numbers	Números ordinales	10
Fractions	fracciones	10
Mathematical Operations	Acciones matemáticas	10
Words involved in calculations	Palabras involucradas en los cálculos	11
Most important Verbs	Verbos más populares	11
Colors	Colores	15
Most Popular Questions	Preguntas más populares	16
Prepositions	Preposiciones	17
ic Introductory Words and Adverbs	Palabras introductorias básicas y adverbios	17
Introductory Words and Adverbs	Palabras introductorias básicas y adverbios	19
Days of the week	Días de la semana	20
Times of Day	Hora del día	21
Seasons	estaciones	22
Words about time	palabras sobre el tiempo	23
The main antonyms	Antónimos clave	25
Geometric shapes	Formas geométricas	26
Measures	Las Medidas	27
Capacities	Las Capacidades	28
Materials	Las Materiales	29
Metalls	Los Metales	30
Human	Humano	31
Anatomy	Anatomía	31

Head	La cabeza	32
Body Parts	Partes del cuerpo	33
Clothes	La ropa	34
outerwear	ropa de abrigo	34
Clothes	La ropa	34
Undergarments	ropa interior	35
Hats	Sombreros	35
Shoes	Zapatos	36
Tissue	Tejido	36
Hygiene and cosmetics	Higiene y cosmética	38
Jewelry	Joyas	39
Watch	Reloj	39
Food	Comida	40
Food	Productos	40
Drinks	Bebidas	42
Vegetables	Verduras	43
Fruits and Nuts	Frutas y nueces	44
Bread and Sweets	Pan y dulces	45
Courses	tribunales	45
Words for eating	Condiciones de la comida	47
Questionnaire	Cuestionario	48
Relatives	parientes	49
Friends and Collegues	Amigos y colegas	50
Words about people	Palabras sobre personas	51
Age	años	51
Children	niñas	52
Feelings	Sentimientos	53
Personal Traits	Rasgos personales	55
Sleep	El Sueño	56
Laugh	Una Risa	57

Communication	comunicación	57
Talk	Una Charla	59
Agreement and Disagreement	Acuerdo y desacuerdo	61

Pronouns — los pronombres

I, me	yo
you	tú
he	él
she	ella
it	el(m), ella(f)
we	nosotros(m), nosotras(f)
you	usted(sing), ustedes(pl), vosotros(m,pl), vosotras(f,pl)
they	ellos(m), ellas(f)

Basic phrases — Frases clave

Hello!	¡Hola!
Hello!	¡Hola!
Good morning!	¡Buenos días!
Good afternoon!	¡Buenas tardes!
Good evening!	¡Buenas noches!
to say hello	decir hola
Hi!	¡Hola!
greeting	saludo (m)
to greet	saludar (vt)
How are you?	¿Cómo estás?
What's new?	¿Qué hay de nuevo?
Bye-Bye! Goodbye!	¡Adiós!
See you soon!	¡Hasta la vista! (fam.)
to say goodbye	¡Hasta pronto!
Cheers!	¡Adiós!
Thank you! Cheers!	¡Gracias!
Thank you very much!	¡Muchas gracias!
My pleasure!	De nada
Don't mention it!	No hay de qué
Excuse me!	¡Perdóname!, ¡Perdóneme! (resp)
to excuse	disculpar (vt)
to apologize	disculparse (vr)
?? apologies	Mis disculpas
I'm sorry!	perdonar (vt)
It's okay!	¡No pasa nada!
please	por favor

Don't forget!	¡No se le olvide!
Certainly!	¡Desde luego!
Of course not!	¡Claro que no!
Okay!	¡De acuerdo!
That's enough!	¡Basta!

How to address a person / Cómo dirigirse a una persona

mister, sir	señor
madam	señora
miss	señorita
young man	joven
young man	niño
miss	niña

Numbers from 0 to 100 / Números de 0 a 100

zero	cero
one	uno
two	dos
three	tres
four	cuatro
five	cinco
six	seis
seven	siete
eight	ocho
nine	nueve
ten	diez
eleven	once
twelve	doce
thirteen	trece
fourteen	catorce
fifteen	quince
sixteen	dieciséis
seventeen	diecisiete
eighteen	dieciocho
nineteen	diecinueve
twenty	veinte
twenty-one	veintiuno

twenty-two	veintidós
twenty-three	veintitrés
thirty	treinta
thirty-one	treinta y uno
thirty-two	treinta y dos
thirty-three	treinta y tres
forty	cuarenta
forty-one	cuarenta y uno
forty-two	cuarenta y dos
forty-three	cuarenta y tres
fifty	cincuenta
fifty-one	cincuenta y uno
fifty-two	cincuenta y dos
fifty-three	cincuenta y tres
sixty	sesenta
sixty-one	sesenta y uno
sixty-two	sesenta y dos
sixty-three	sesenta y tres
seventy	setenta
seventy-one	setenta y uno
seventy-two	setenta y dos
seventy-three	setenta y tres
eighty	ochenta
eighty-one	ochenta y uno
eighty-two	ochenta y dos
eighty-three	ochenta y tres
ninety	noventa
ninety-one	noventa y uno
ninety-two	noventa y dos
ninety-three	noventa y tres

Numbers from 100 to milliard — Números de 100 a mil millones

one hundred	cien
two hundred	doscientos
three hundred	trescientos
four hundred	cuatrocientos
five hundred	quinientos
six hundred	seiscientos

seven hundred	setecientos
eight hundred	ochocientos
nine hundred	novecientos
thousand	mil
two thousand	dos mil
three thousand	tres mil
ten thousand	diez mil
one hundred thousand	cien mil
million	millón (m)
billion	mil millones

Ordinal Numbers — Números ordinales

first	primero (adj)
second	segundo (adj)
third	tercero (adj)
fourth	cuarto (adj)
fifth	quinto (adj)
sixth	Sexto (adj)
seventh	séptimo (adj)
eighth	octavo (adj)
ninth	noveno (adj)
tenth	décimo (adj)

Fractions — fracciones

fraction	fracción (f)
one half	un medio
one third	un tercio
one quarter	un cuarto
one eighth	un octavo
one tenth	un décimo
two thirds	dos tercios
three quarters	tres cuartos

Mathematical Operations — Acciones matemáticas

subtraction	sustracción (f)
to subtract	sustraer (vt)

division	división (f)
to divide	dividir (vt)
addition	adición (f)
to add up	sumar (vt)
to add	sumar (vt)
multiplication	multiplicación (f)
to multiply	multiplicar (vt)

Words involved in calculations — Palabras involucradas en los cálculos

figure	cifra (f)
number	número (m)
numeral	numeral (m)
minus	menos (m)
plus	más (m)
formula	fórmula (f)
calculation	cálculo (m)
to count	contar (vt)
to compare	calcular (vt)
How much?	comparar (vt)
How many?	¿cuánto?
sum, total	suma (f)
result	resultado (m)
remainder	resto (m)
a few ...	unos pocos
few ...	poco (adv)
the rest	resto (m)
one and a half	uno y medio
dozen	docena (í)
in half	en dos partes
equally	en partes iguales
half	mitad (f)
time	vez (f)

Most important Verbs — Verbos más populares

to run	correr (vi)
to be afraid	tener miedo
to take	tomar (vt)

to be	estar (vi), ser (vi)
to see	ver (vt)
to own	poseer (vt)
to object	objetar (vt)
to come in	entrar (vi)
to choose	escoger (vt)
to go out	salir (vi)
to speak	hablar (vi, vt)
to cook	preparar (vt)
to give	dar (vt)
to do	hacer (vt)
to trust	confiar (vt)
to think	pensar (vi, vt)
to complain	quejarse (vr)
to wait	esperar (vt)
to forget	olvidar (vt)
to have breakfast	desayunar (vi)
to order	pedir (vt)
to finish	terminar (vt)
to notice	notar (vt)
to write down	tomar nota
to defend	defender (vt)
to call	llamar (vt)
to know	conocer (vt)
to know	saber (vt)
to play	jugar (vi)
to go	ir (vi)
to excuse	disculpar (vt)
to change	cambiar (vt)
to study	estudiar (vt)
to have	tener (vt)
to be interested in ...	interesarse (vr)
to inform	informar (vt)
to look for ...	buscar (vt)
to control	controlar (vt)
to steal	robar (vt)
to shout	gritar (vi)
to go for a swim	bañarse (vr)
to fly	volar (vi)
to catch	coger (vt)

to break	romper (vt)
to love	querer (vt)
to pray	orar (vi)
to keep silent	callarse (vr)
can	poder (v aux)
to observe	observar (vt)
to hope	esperar (vt)
to punish	castigar (vt)
to insist	insistir (vi)
to find	encontrar (vt)
to begin	comenzar (vi, vt)
to underestimate	subestimar (vt)
to fancy	gustar (vi)
to have lunch	almorzar (vi)
to promise	prometer (vt)
to deceive	engañar (vi, vt)
to discuss	discutir (vt)
to unite	unir (vt)
to explain	explicar (vt)
to mean	significar (vt)
to liberate	liberar (vt)
to insult	insultar (vt)
to stop	pararse (vr)
to answer	responder (vi, vt)
to guess right	adivinar (vt)
to refuse	negarse (vr)
to open	abrir (vt)
to send	enviar (vt)
to hunt	cazar (vi, vt)
to make a mistake	equivocarse (vr)
to fall	caer (vi)
to translate	traducir (vt)
to write	escribir (vt)
to swim	nadar (vi)
to cry	llorar (vi)
to plan	planear (vt)
to pay	pagar (vi, vt)
to turn	girar (vi)
to repeat	repetir (vt)
to sign	firmar (vt)

to give a hint	dar una pista
to show	mostrar (vt)
to help	ayudar (vt)
to understand	comprender (vt)
to expect	prever (vt)
to propose	proponer (vt)
to prefer	preferir (vt)
to warn	advertir (vt)
to stop	cesar (vt)
to invite	invitar (vt)
to arrive	llegar (vi)
to order	ordenar (vt)
to belong to ...	pertenecerá ...
to try	tratar de ...
to sell	vender (vt)
to continue	continuar (vt)
to pronounce	pronunciar (vt)
to miss	faltar a ...
to ask	pedir (vt)
to forgive	perdonar (vt)
to hide	esconder (vt)
to confuse, to mix up	confundir (vt)
to work	trabajar (vi)
to permit	permitir (vt)
to count on ...	contar con ...
to reserve, to book	reservar (vt)
to recommend	recomendar (vt)
to drop	dejar caer
to scold	regañar (vt)
to run, to manage	dirigir (vt)
to dig	cavar (vt)
to sit down	sentarse (vr)
to say	decir (vt)
to follow ...	seguir ...
to hear	oír (vt)
to laugh	reírse (vr)
to rent	alquilar (vt)
to advise	aconsejar (vt)
to agree	estar de acuerdo
to regret	arrepentirse (vr)

to create	crear (vt)
to doubt	dudar (vt)
to keep	guardar (vt)
to save, to rescue	salvar (vt)
to ask	preguntar (vt)
to come down	descender (vi)
to compare	comparar (vt)
to cost	costar (vt)
to shoot	tirar (vi)
to exist	existir (vi)
to count	contar (vt)
to hurry	darse prisa
to demand	exigir (vt)
to be needed	ser necesario
to touch	tocar (vt)
to kill	matar (vt)
to threaten	amenazar (vt)
to be surprised	sorprenderse (vr)
to have dinner	cenar (vi)
to decorate	decorar (vt)
to smile	sonreír (vi)
to mention	mencionar (vt)
to participate	participar (vi)
to boast	alabarse (vr)
to want	querer (vt)
to be hungry	tener hambre
to be thirsty	tener sed
to read	leer (vi, vt)
to joke	bromear (vi)

Colors / Colores

colour	color (m)
shade	matiz (m)
hue	tono (m)
rainbow	arco (m) iris
white	blanco (adj)
black	negro (adj)
grey	gris (adj)
green	verde (adj)

yellow	amarillo (adj)
red	rojo (adj)
blue	azul (adj)
light blue	azul claro (adj)
pink	rosado (adj)
orange	anaranjado (adj)
violet	violeta (adj)
brown	marrón (adj)
golden	dorado (adj)
silvery	argentado (adj)
beige	beige (adj)
cream	crema (adj)
turquoise	turquesa (adj)
cherry red	rojo cereza (adj)
lilac	lila (adj)
crimson	carmesí (adj)
light	Claro (adj)
dark	oscuro (adj)
bright	vivo (adj)
coloured	de color (adj)
colour	en colores (adj)
black-and-white	blanco y negro (adj)
plain	unicolor (adj)
multicoloured	multicolor (adj)

Most Popular Questions   Preguntas más populares

Who?	¿Quién?
What?	¿Qué?
Where?	¿Dónde?
Where?	¿A dónde?
Where ... from?	¿De dónde?
When?	¿Cuándo?
Why?	¿Para qué?
What for?	¿Por qué? , ¿Por qué razón?
How?	¿Cómo?
Which?	¿Cuál?
To whom?	¿A quién?
About whom?	¿De quién?

About what?	¿De qué?
With whom?	¿Con quién?
How many?	¿Cuánto?
How much?	¿Cuánto?
Whose?	¿De quién?

Prepositions — Preposiciones

with	con
without	sin
to	a
about	de
before	antes de ...
under	debajo de ...
above	sobre ...
on	en, sobre
from	de
of	de
in	dentro de ...
over	encima de ...

ic Introductory Words and Adverbs — Palabras introductorias básicas y adverbios

Where?	¿Dónde?
here	aquí (adv)
there	allí (adv)
somewhere	en alguna parte
nowhere	en ninguna parte
by	junto a ...
by the window	junto a la ventana
Where?	¿A dónde?
here	aquí (adv)
there	allí (adv)
from here	de aquí (adv)
from there	de allí (adv)
close	cerca
far	lejos (adv)
not far	no lejos
left	izquierdo (adj)

on the left	a la izquierda
to the left	a la izquierda
right	derecho (adj)
on the right	a la derecha
to the right	a la derecha
in front	delante
front	delantero (adj)
ahead	adelante
behind	detrás de ...
from behind	desde atrás
back	atrás
middle	centro (m), medio (m)
in the middle	en medio (adv)
at the side	de costado (adv)
everywhere	en todas partes
around	alrededor (adv)
from inside	de dentro (adv)
somewhere	a alguna parte
straight	todo derecho (adv)
back	atrás
from anywhere	de alguna parte (adv)
from somewhere	no se sabe de dónde
firstly	en primer lugar
secondly	segundo (adv)
thirdly	tercero
suddenly	de súbito
at first	al principio (adv)
for the first time	por primera vez
long before ...	mucho tiempo antes ...
for good	para siempre (adv)
never	jamás (adv)
again	de nuevo (adv)
now	ahora (adv)
often	a menudo (adv)
then	entonces (adv)
urgently	urgentemente
usually	normalmente (adv)
by the way, ...	a propósito
possible	es probable
probably	probablemente

maybe	es posible
besides ...	además ...
that's why ...	por eso ...
in spite of...	a pesar de ...
thanks to ...	gracias a ...
what	qué
that	que
something	algo
anything, something	algo
nothing	nada
who	quien
someone	alguien
somebody	alguien
nobody	nadie
nowhere	a ninguna parte
nobody's	de nadie
somebody's	de alguien
so	asi que…
also	además ...
too	también

Introductory Words and Adverbs   Palabras introductorias básicas y adverbios

Why?	¿Por qué?
for some reason	no se sabe porqué
because ...	porque ...
and	para algo (adv)
or	?
but	o
for	para
too	demasiado (adv)
only	sólo (adv)
exactly	exactamente (adv)
about	unos ...
approximately	aproximadamente
approximate	aproximado (adj)
almost	casi (adv)
the rest	resto (m)
the other	el otro

other	otro
each	cada (adj)
any	cada (adj)
much	cualquier (adj)
many	mucho (adv)
many people	muchos
all	todos
in exchange for…	a cambio de …
in exchange	en cambio (adv)
by hand	a mano
hardly	es poco probable
probably	probablemente
on purpose	a propósito (adv)
by accident	por accidente (adv)
very	muy (adv)
for example	por ejemplo (adv)
between	entre
among	entre
so much	tan, tanto
especially	especialmente (adv)

Days of the week — Días de la semana

Monday	lunes (m)
Tuesday	martes (m)
Wednesday	miércoles (m)
Thursday	jueves (m)
Friday	viernes (m)
Saturday	sábado (m)
Sunday	domingo (m)
today	hoy (adv)
tomorrow	mañana (adv)
the day after tomorrow	pasado mañana
yesterday	ayer (adv)
the day before yesterday	anteayer (adv)
day	día (m)
working day	día (m) de trabajo
public holiday	día (m) de fiesta
day off	día (m) de descanso
weekend	fin (m) de semana

all day long	todo el día
next day	al día siguiente
two days ago	dos días atrás
the day before	en vísperas (adv)
daily	diario (adj)
every day	cada dia (adv)
week	semana (f)
last week	semana (f) pasada
next week	semana (f) que viene
weekly	semanal (adj)
every week	cada semana (adv)
twice a week	dos veces por semana
every Tuesday	todos los martes

Times of Day — Hora del día

morning	mañana (f)
in the morning	por la mañana
noon, midday	mediodía (m)
in the afternoon	por la tarde
evening	tarde (?)
in the evening	por la noche
night	noche (f)
at night	por la noche
midnight	medianoche (f)
second	segundo (m)
minute	minuto (m)
hour	hora (f)
half an hour	media hora (f)
quarter of an hour	cuarto (m) de hora
fifteen minutes	quince minutos
twenty four hours	veinticuatro horas(fpl)
sunrise	salida(m)del sol
dawn	amanecer (m)
early morning	madrugada(f)
sunset	puesta (f) del sol
early in the morning	por la mañana temprano
today in the morning	esta mañana
tomorrow moning	mañana por la mañana
this afternoon	esta tarde

in the afternoon	por la tarde
tomorrow afternoon	mañana por la tarde
tonight	esta tarde, esta noche
tomorrow night	mañana por la noche
at 3 o'clock sharp	a las tres en punto
about 4 o'clock	a eso de las cuatro
by 12 o'clock	para las doce
in 20 minutes	dentro de veinte minutos
in an hour	dentro de una hora
on time	a tiempo (adv)
a quaretr to…	... menos cuarto
withing an hour	durante una hora
every 15 minutes	cada quince minutos
round the clock	día y noche

Seasons — estaciones

January	enero (m)
February	febrero (m)
March	marzo (m)
April	abril (m)
May	mayo (m)
June	junio (m)
July	julio (m)
August	agosto (m)
September	septiembre (m)
October	octubre (m)
November	noviembre (m)
December	diciembre (m)
spring	primavera (f)
in spring	en primavera
spring	de primavera (adj)
summer	verano (m)
in summer	en verano
summer	de verano (adj)
autumn	otoño (m)
in autumn	en otoño
autumn	de otoño (adj)
winter	invierno (m)
in winter	en invierno

winter	de invierno (adj)
month	mes (m)
this month	este mes
next month	al mes siguiente
last month	el mes pasado
a month ago	mes (m)
in a month	este mes???
in two months	al mes siguiente
a whole month	el mes pasado
all month long	hace un mes
monthly	mensual
bi-monthly	bimensual
every month	cada mes
twice a month	todo un mes??
year	año (m)
this year	este año
next year	el próximo año
last year	el año pasado
a year ago	hace un año
in a year	dentro de un año
in two years	dentro de dos años
a whole year	todo el año
all year long	todo un año
every year	cada año
annual	anual (adj)
annually	anualmente (adv)
4 times a year	cuatro veces por año
date	fecha (f), día (m)
date	fecha (f)
calendar	calendario (m)
half a year	medio año (m)
six months	ocho meses
season	temporada (f)
century	siglo (m)

Words about time — palabras sobre el tiempo

time	tiempo (m)
instant	instante (m)

instant	instantáneo (adj)
period	lapso (m) de tiempo
life	vida (f)
eternity	eternidad (f)
epoch	época (f)
era	era (f)
cycle	ciclo (m)
term , period	período (m)
the future	futuro (m)
future	que viene (adj)
next time	la próxima vez
the past	pasado (m)
past	pasado (adj)
last time	la última vez
later	más tarde (adv)
after	después
nowadays	actualmente (adv)
now	ahora (adv)
immediately	inmediatamente
soon	pronto (adv)
in advance	de antemano (adv)
a long time ago	hace mucho (adv)
recently	hace poco (adv)
destiny	destino (m)
memories	recuerdos (mpl)
archives	archivo (m)
during ...	durante ...
long, a long time	mucho tiempo (adv)
not long	poco tiempo (adv)
early	temprano (adv)
late	tarde (adv)
forever	para siempre (adv)
to start	comenzar (vt)
to postpone	aplazar (vt)
at the same time	simultáneamente
permanently	permanentemente
constant	Constante (adj)
temporary	temporal (adj)
sometimes	a veces (adv)
rarely	rara vez (adv)

often	a menudo (adv)

The main antonyms / Antónimos clave

rich	rico (adj)
poor	pobre (adj)
ill, sick	enfermo (adj)
healthy	sano (adj)
big	grande (adj)
small	pequeño (adj)
quickly	rápidamente (adv)
slowly	lentamente (adv)
fast	rápido (adj)
slow	lento (adj)
cheerful	alegre (adj)
sad	triste (adj)
together	juntos (adv)
separately	separadamente (adv)
aloud	en voz alta
silently	en silencio
tall	alto (adj)
low	bajo (adj)
deep	profundo (adj)
shallow	poco profundo (adj)
yes	Sí
no	no
distant	lejano (adj)
nearby	cercano (adj)
far	lejos (adv)
nearby	cerco (adv)
long	largo (adj)
short	corto (adj)
good	bueno (adj)
evil	malvado (adj)
married	casado (adj)
single	soltero (adj)
to forbid	prohibir (vt)
to permit	permitir (vt)
end	fin (m)
beginning	principio (m)

left	izquierdo (adj)
right	derecho (adj)
first	primero (adj)
last	último (adj)
crime	crimen (m)
punishment	castigo (m)
to order	ordenar (vt)
to obey	obedecer (vi, vt)
straight	recto (adj)
curved	curvo (adj)
heaven	paraíso (m)
hell	infierno (m)
to be born	nacer (vi)
to die	morir (vi)
strong	fuerte (adj)
weak	débil (adj)
old	viejo (adj)
young	joven (adj)
old	viejo (adj)
new	nuevo (adj)
hard	duro (adj)
soft	blando (adj)
warm	cálido (adj)
cold	frío (adj)
fat	gordo (adj)
slim	delgado (adj)
narrow	estrecho (adj)
wide	ancho (adj)
good	bueno (adj)
bad	malo (adj)
brave	valiente (adj)
cowardly	cobarde (adj)

Geometric shapes — Formas geométricas

square	cuadrado (m)
square	cuadrado (adj)
circle	círculo (m)
round	redondo (adj)
triangle	triángulo (m)

triangular	triangular (adj)
oval	óvalo (m)
oval	oval (adj)
rectangle	rectángulo (m)
rectangular	rectangular (adj)
pyramid	pirámide (f)
rhombus	rombo (m)
trapezium	trapecio (m)
cube	cubo (m)
prism	prisma (m)
circumference	circunferencia (f)
sphere	esfera (f)
globe	globo (m)
diameter	diámetro (m)
radius	radio (f)
perimeter	perímetro (m)
centre	centro (m)
horizontal	horizontal (adj)
vertical	vertical (adj)
parallel	paralela (f)
parallel	paralelo (adj)
line	linea (f)
stroke	trazo (m)
straight line	recta (f)
curve	curva (f)
thin	fino (adj)
contour	contorno (m)
intersection	intersección (m)
right angle	ángulo (m) recto
segment	segmento (m)
sector	sector (m)
side	lado (m)
angle	ángulo (m)

Measures — Las Medidas

weight	peso (m)
length	longitud (f)
width	anchura (f)
height	altura (f)

depth	profundidad (f)
volume	volumen (m)
area	superficie (f), área (f)
gram	gramo (m)
milligram	miligramo (m)
kilogram	kilogramo (m)
ton	tonelada (f)
pound	libra (f)
ounce	onza (f)
metre	metro (m)
millimetre	milímetro (m)
centimetre	centímetro (m)
kilometre	kilómetro (m)
mile	milla (f)
inch	pulgada (f)
foot	pie (m)
yard	yarda (f)
square metre	metro (m) cuadrado
hectare	hectárea (f)
litre	litro (m)
degree	grado (m)
volt	voltio (m)
ampere	amperio (m)
horsepower	caballo (m) de fuerza
quantity	cantidad (f)
a little bit of ...	un poco de ...
half	mitad (f)
dozen	docena (f)
piece	pieza (f)
size	dimensión (f)
scale	escala (f)
minimum	mínimo (adj)
the smallest	el menor (adj)
medium	medio (adj)
maximum	máximo (adj)
the largest	el más grande (adj)

Capacities — Las Capacidades

jar	tarro (m) de vidrio

tin	lata (f)
bucket	cubo (m)
barrel	barril (m)
basin	palangana (f)
tank	tanque (m)
hip flask	petaca (f)
jerry can	bidón (m) de gasolina
cistern	cisterna (f)
mug	taza (f)
cup	taza (f)
saucer	platillo (m)
glass (tumbler)	vaso (m)
glass	copa (f)
stew pot	cacerola (f)
bottle	botella (f)
neck	cuello (m) de botella
carafe	garrafa (f)
jug	jarro (m)
vessel	recipiente (m)
pot	olla (f)
vase	florero (m)
bottle	frasco (m)
vial, small bottle	frasquito (m)
tube	tubo (m)
sack (bag)	saco (m)
bag	bolsa (f)
packet	paquete (m)
box	caja (f)
box	cajón (m)
basket	cesta (f)

Materials / Las Materiales

material	material (f)
wood	madera (f)
wooden	de madera (?dj)
glass	Cristal (m)
glass	de cristal (adj
stone	piedra (f)
stone	de piedra (adj)

plastic	plástico (m)
plastic	de plástico(adj)
rubber	goma (f)
rubber	de goma(adj)
material, fabric	tela (m)
fabric	de tela(adj)
paper	papel (m)
paper	de papel(adj)
cardboard	Cartón (m)
cardboard	de cartón(adj)
polythene	polietileno (m)
cellophane	celofán (m)
linoleum	linóleo (m)
plywood	chapa (f) de madera
porcelain	porcelana (f)
porcelain	de porcelana(adj)
clay	arcilla (f)
clay	de arcilla(adj)
ceramics	cerámica m
ceramic	de cerámica(adj)

Metalls / Los Metales

metal	metal (m)
metal	de metal (?®)
alloy	aleación (f)
gold	oro (m)
gold, golden	de oro (adj)
silver	plata (f)
silver	de plata (adj)
iron	hierro (m)
iron, made of iron	de hierro (adj)
steel	acero (m)
steel	de acero (adj)
copper	cobre (m)
copper	de cobre (adj)
aluminium	aluminio (m)
aluminium	de aluminio
bronze	bronce (m)
bronze	de bronce

brass	latón (m)
nickel	níquel (m)
platinum	platino (m)
mercury	mercurio (m)
tin	estaño (m)
lead	plomo (m)
zinc	zinc (m)

Human / Humano

human being	ser (m) humano
man	hombre (m)
woman	mujer (f)
child	niño -a (m, f)
girl	niña (f)
boy	niño (m)
teenager	adolescente (m)
old man	anciano (m)
old woman	anciana (f)

Anatomy / Anatomía

organism	organismo (m)
heart	corazón (m)
blood	sangre (f)
artery	arteria (f)
vein	vena (f)
brain	cerebro (m)
nerve	nervio (m)
nerves	nervios (mpl)
vertebra	vértebra (f)
spine	columna (f) vertebral
stomach	estómago (m)
intestines	intestinos (mpl)
intestine	intestino (m)
liver	hígado (m)
kidney	riñón (m)
bone	hueso (m)
skeleton	esqueleto (m)
rib	costilla (f)
skull	cráneo (m)

muscle	músculo (m)
biceps	bíceps (m)
triceps	tríceps (m)
tendon	tendón (m)
joint	articulación (f)
lungs	pulmones (mpl)
genitals	genitales (mpl)
skin	piel (f)

Head — La cabeza

head	cabeza (f)
face	cara (f)
nose	nariz (f)
mouth	boca (f)
eye	ojo (m)
eyes	ojos (mpl)
pupil	pupila (f)
eyebrow	ceja (f)
eyelash	pestaña (f)
eyelid	párpado (m)
tongue	lengua (f)
tooth	diente (m)
lips	labios (mpl)
cheekbones	pómulos (mpl)
gum	encía (f)
palate	paladar (m)
nostrils	ventanas (fpl)
chin	mentón (m)
jaw	mandíbula (f)
cheek	mejilla (f)
forehead	frente (f)
temple	sien (f)
ear	oreja (f)
back of the head	nuca (f)
neck	cuello (m)
throat	garganta (f)
hair	cabello (m)
hairstyle	peinado (m)
haircut	corte (m) de pelo

wig	peluca (f)
moustache	bigotes (mpl)
beard	barba (f)
to have	tener (vt)
plait	trenza (f)
sideboards	patillas (fpl)
red-haired	pelirrojo (adj)
grey	canoso fadjj
bald	calvo (adj)
bald patch	calva (f)
ponytail	cola (f) de caballo
fringe	flequillo (m)

Body Parts — Partes del cuerpo

hand	mano (f)
arm	brazo (m)
finger	dedo (m)
thumb	dedo (m) pulgar
little finger	dedo (m) meñique
nail	uña (f)
fist	puño (m)
palm	palma(f)
wrist	muñeca (f)
forearm	antebrazo (m)
elbow	codo(m)
shoulder	hombro (m)
leg	pierna (f)
foot	planta (f)
knee	rodilla (f)
calf	pantorrilla (f)
hip	cadera (f)
heel	talón (m)
body	cuerpo (m)
stomach	vientre (m)
chest	pecho (m)
breast	seno (m)
flank	lado (m), costado (m)
back	espalda (f)
lower back	cintura (f)

waist	talle (m)
navel	ombligo (m)
buttocks	nalgas (fpl)
bottom	trasero (m)
beauty mark	lunar (m) , marca (f) de nacimiento
tattoo	tatuaje (m)
scar	cicatriz (f)

Clothes — La ropa

outerwear — ropa de abrigo

clothes	ropa (f), vestido (m)
outer clothing	ropa (f) de calle
winter clothing	ropa (f) de invierno
overcoat	abrigo (m)
fur coat	abrigo (m) de piel
fur jacket	abrigo (m) corto de piel
down coat	plumón (m)
jacket	cazadora (f)
raincoat	impermeable (m)
waterproof	impermeable (adj)

Clothes — La ropa

shirt	camisa (f)
trousers	pantalones (mpl)
jeans	vaqueros (mpl)
jacket	chaqueta (f), saco (m)
suit	traje (m)
dress	vestido (m)
skirt	falda (f)
blouse	blusa (f)
knitted jacket	rebeca (f)
jacket	chaqueta (f)
T-shirt	camiseta (f)
shorts	pantalón (m) corto
tracksuit	traje (m) deportivo
bathrobe	bata (f) de baño
pyjamas	pijama (f)

sweater	jersey (m), suéter (m)
pullover	pulóver (m)
waistcoat	chaleco (m)
tailcoat	frac (m)
dinner suit	esmoquin (m)
uniform	uniforme (m)
work wear	ropa (f) de trabajo
boiler suit	mono (m)
coat	bata (f) blanca

Undergarments — ropa interior

underwear	ropa (f) interior
vest	camiseta (f) interior
socks	calcetines (mpl)
nightgown	camisón (m)
bra	sostén (m)
knee highs	calcetines (mpl) altos
tights	leotardos (mpl)
stockings	medias (fpl)
swimsuit, bikini	traje (m) de baño

Hats — Sombreros

hat	gorro (m)
trilby hat	sombrero (m)
baseball cap	gorra (f) de béisbol
flatcap	gorra (f) plana
beret	boina (f)
hood	capuchón (m)
panama	panamá (m)
knitted hat	gorro (m) de punto
headscarf	pañuelo (m)
women's hat	sombrero (m) femenino
hard hat	casco (m)
forage cap	gorro (m) de campaña
helmet	casco (m)
bowler	bombín (m)
top hat	sombrero (m) de copa

Shoes — Zapatos

footwear	calzado (m)
ankle boots	botas (fpl)
shoes	zapatos (mpl)
boots	zapatos (mpl)
slippers	zapatillas (fpl)
trainers	zapatos (mpl) de tenis
plimsolls, pumps	zapatos (mpl) deportivos
sandals	sandalias (fpl)
cobbler	zapatero (m)
heel	tacón (m)
pair	par (m)
shoelace	cordón (m)
to lace up	encordonar (vt)
shoehorn	calzador (m)
shoe polish	betún (m)

Tissue — Tejido

cotton	algodón (m)
cotton	de algodón (adj)!!!
flax	lino
flax	de lino
silk	seda (f)
silk	de seda (adj)
wool	lana (f)
woollen	de lana (adj)!!!
velvet	terciopelo (m)
suede	gamuza (f)
corduroy	pana (f)
nylon	nylon (m)
nylon	de nylon (adj)
polyester	poliéster (m)
polyester	de poliéster (adj)
leather	cuero (m)
leather	de cuero
fur	piel (f)
fur	de piel
gloves	guantes (mpl)

mittens	manoplas (fpl)
scarf	bufanda (f)
glasses	gafas (fpl)
frame	montura (f)
umbrella	paraguas (m)
walking stick	bastón (m)
hairbrush	cepillo (m) de pelo
fan	abanico (m)
tie	corbata (f)
bow tie	pajarita (f)
braces	tirantes (mpl)
handkerchief	moquero (m)
comb	peine (m)
hair slide	pasador (m)
hairpin	horquilla (m)
buckle	hebilla (f)
belt	cinturón (m)
shoulder strap	correa (f)
bag	bolsa (f)
handbag	bolso (m)
rucksack	mochila (f)
fashion	moda (f)
in vogue	de moda
fashion designer	diseñador (m) de modas
collar	cuello (m)
pocket	bolsillo (m)
pocket	de bolsillo (adj)
sleeve	manga (f)
hanging loop	colgador (m)
flies	bragueta (m)
zip	cremallera (f)
fastener	cierre (m)
button	botón (m)
buttonhole	ojal (m)
to come off	saltar (vi)
to sew	coser (vi, vt)
to embroider	bordar (vt)
embroidery	bordado (m)
sewing needle	aguja (f)
thread	hilo (m)

seam	costura (f)
to get dirty	ensuciarse (vr)
stain	mancha (f)
to crease, crumple	arrugarse (vr)
to tear	rasgar (vt)
clothes moth	polilla (f)

Hygiene and cosmetics / Higiene y cosmética

toothpaste	pasta (f) de dientes
toothbrush	cepillo (m) de dientes
to clean one's teeth	limpiarse los dientes
razor	maquinilla (f) de afeitar
shaving cream	crema (f) de afeitar
to shave	afeitarse
soap	jabon (m)
shampoo	champu (m)
scissors	tijeras (fpl)
nail file	lima (f) de unas
nail clippers	cortaunas (mpl)
tweezers	pinzas (fpl)
cosmetics	cosmeticos (mpl)
face mask	mascarilla (f)
manicure	manicura (f)
to have a manicure	hacer la manicura
pedicure	pedicura (f)
make-up bag	neceser (m) de maquillaje
face powder	polvos (mpl), polvera (f)
powder compact	colorete (m), rubor (m)
blusher	rubor (m)
perfume	perfume (m)
toilet water	agua (f) perfumada
lotion	loción (f)
cologne	agua (f) de colonia
eyeshadow	sombra (f) de ojos
eyeliner	lápiz (m) de ojos
mascara	rímel (m)
lipstick	pintalabios (m)
nail polish	esmalte (m) de uñas
hair spray	fijador (m) (para el pelo)

deodorant	desodorante (m)
cream	crema (f)
face cream	crema (f) de belleza
hand cream	crema (f) de manos
anti-wrinkle cream	crema (f) antiarrugas
day cream	crema (f) de dia
night cream	crema (f) de noche
tampon	tampón (m)
toilet paper	papel (m) higiénico
hair dryer	secador (m) de pelo

Jewelry — Joyas

jewellery	joyas (fpl)
precious	precioso (adj)
hallmark	contraste (m)
ring	anillo (m)
wedding ring	anillo (m) de boda
bracelet	pulsera (f)
earrings	pendientes (mpl)
necklace	collar (m)
crown	corona (f)
bead necklace	collar (m) de abalorios
diamond	diamante (m)
emerald	esmeralda (f)
ruby	rubí (m)
sapphire	zafiro (m)
pearl	perla (f)
amber	ámbar (m)

Watch — Reloj

watch	reloj (m)
dial	esfera (f)
hand	aguja (f)
bracelet	pulsera (f)
watch strap	correa (f)
battery	pila (f)
to be flat	descargarse (vr)
to change a battery	cambiar la pila
to run fast	adelantarse (vr)

to run slow	retrasarse (vr)
wall clock	reloj (m) de pared
hourglass	reloj (m) de arena
sundial	reloj (m) de sol
alarm clock	despertador (m)
watchmaker	relojero (m)
to repair	reparar (vt)

Food — Comida

Food — Productos

meat	carne (f)
chicken	gallina (f)
young chicken	pollo (m)
duck	pato (m)
goose	ganso (m)
game	caza (f) menor
turkey	pava (f)
pork	carne (f) de cerdo
veal	carne (f) de ternera
lamb	carne (f) de carnero
beef	carne (f) de vaca
rabbit	conejo (m)
sausage	salchichón (m)
Vienna sausage	salchicha (f)
bacon	beicon (m)
ham	jamón (m)
gammon	jamón (m) fresco
pate	paté (m)
liver	hígado (m)
lard	tocino (m)
mince	carne (f) picada
tongue	lengua (m)
egg	huevo (m)
eggs	huevos (mpl)
egg white	clara (f)
egg yolk	yema (f)
fish	pescado (m)
seafood	mariscos (mpl)

crustaceans	crustáceos (mpl)
caviar	caviar (m)
crab	cangrejo (m) de mar
prawn	camarón (m)
oyster	ostra (f)
spiny lobster	langosta (f)
octopus	pulpo (m)
squid	calamar (m)
sturgeon	esturión (m)
salmon	salmón (m)
halibut	fletán (m)
cod	bacalao (m)
mackerel	caballa (f)
tuna	atún (m)
eel	anguila (f)
trout	trucha (f)
sardine	sardina (f)
pike	lucio (m)
herring	arenque (m)
bread	pan (m)
cheese	queso (m)
sugar	azúcar (m)
salt	sal (f)
rice	arroz (m)
pasta	macarrones (mpl)
noodles	tallarines (mpl)
butter	mantequilla (f)
vegetable oil	aceite (m) vegetal
sunflower oil	aceite (m) de girasol
margarine	margarina (f)
olives	olivas (fpl)
olive oil	aceite (m) de oliva
milk	leche (f)
condensed milk	leche (f) condensada
yogurt	yogur (m)
sour cream	nata (f) agria
cream	nata (f) líquida
mayonnaise	mayonesa (f)
buttercream	crema (f) de mantequilla
groats	cereal molido grueso

flour	harina (f)
tinned food	conservas (fpl)
cornflakes	copos (mpl) de maíz
honey	miel (f)
jam	confitura (f)
chewing gum	chicle (m)

Drinks / Bebidas

water	agua (f)
drinking water	agua (f)
mineral water	agua (f) mineral
still	sin gas
carbonated	gaseoso (adj)
sparkling	con gas
ice	hielo (m)
with ice	con hielo
non-alcoholic	sin alcohol
soft drink	bebida (f) sin alcohol
cool soft drink	refresco (m)
lemonade	limonada (f)
spirits	bebidas (fpl) alcohólicas
wine	Vino (m)
white wine	vino (m) blanco
red wine	vino (m) tinto
liqueur	licor (m)
champagne	champaña (f)
vermouth	vermú (m)
whisky	Whisky (m)
vodka	vodka (m)
gin	ginebra (f)
cognac	coñac (m)
rum	ron (m)
coffee	café (m)
black coffee	café (m) solo
white coffee	café (m) con leche
cappuccino	capuchino (m)
instant coffee	café (m) soluble
milk	leche (f)
cocktail	cóctel (m)

milk shake	batido (m)
juice	zumo (m)
tomato juice	jugo (m) de tomate
orange juice	zumo (m) de naranja
freshly squeezed juice	jugo (m) fresco
beer	cerveza (f)
lager	cerveza (f) rubia
bitter!!!	cerveza (f) negra
tea	té (m)
black tea	té (m) negro
green tea	té (m) verde

Vegetables / Verduras

vegetables	verduras (fpl)
greens	legumbres (mpl)
tomato	tomate (m)
cucumber	pepino (m)
carrot	zanahoria (f)
potato	patata m
onion	cebolla (f)
garlic	ajo (m)
cabbage	col (f)
cauliflower	coliflor (f)
Brussels sprouts	col (f) de Bruselas
broccoli	bròcoli (m)
beetroot	remolacha (f)
aubergine	berenjena (f)
marrow??	calabacín (m)
pumpkin	calabaza (f)
turnip	nabo (m)
parsley	perejil (m)
dill	eneldo (m)
lettuce	lechuga m
celery	apio (m)
asparagus	espárrago (m)
spinach	espinaca (f)
pea	guisante (m)
beans	habas (fpl)
maize	maíz (m)

kidney bean	fréjol (m)
bell pepper	pimentón (m)
radish	rábano (m)
artichoke	alcachofa cf)

Fruits and Nuts / Frutas y nueces

fruit	fruto (m)
apple	manzana (f)
pear	pera (f)
lemon	limón (m)
orange	naranja (f)
strawberry	fresa (f)
tangerine	mandarina (f)
plum	ciruela (f)
peach	melocotón (m)
apricot	albaricoque (m)
raspberry	frambuesa (fj
pineapple	ananás (m)
banana	banana (f)
watermelon	sandía (f)
grape	uva (f)
sour cherry	guinda (f)
sweet cherry	cereza (f)
melon	melón (m)
grapefruit	pomelo (m)
avocado	aguacate (m)
papaya	papaya (m)
mango	mango (m)
pomegranate	granada (f)
redcurrant	grosella (f) roja
blackcurrant	grosella ? negra
gooseberry	grosella ? espinosa
bilberry	arándano (m)
blackberry	zarzamoras (fpl)
raisin	pasas(fpl)
fig	higo (m)
date	dátil (m)
peanut	cacahuete (m)
almond	almendra ?

walnut	nuez (f)
hazelnut	avellana (f)
coconut	nuez (f) de coco
pistachios	pistachos (mpl)

Bread and Sweets — Pan y dulces

confectionery	pasteles (mpl)
bread	pan (m)
biscuits	galletas (fpl)
chocolate	chocolate (m)
chocolate	de chocolate (adj)
sweet	caramelo (m)
cake	tarta (f)
cake	tarta (f)
pie	pastel (m)
filling	relleno (m)
jam	confitura (f)
marmalade	mermelada (f)
waffle	gofre (m)
ice-cream	helado (m)
pudding	pudín (f)

Courses — tribunales

course, dish	plato (m)
cuisine	cocina (f)
recipe	receta (f)
portion	porción (f)
salad	ensalada (f)
soup	sopa (f)
clear soup	caldo (m)
sandwich	bocadillo (m)
fried eggs	huevos (mpl) fritos
cutlet	chuleta (f)
hamburger	hamburguesa (f)
steak	bistec (m)
roast meat	asado (m)
garnish	guarnición (f)
spaghetti	espagueti (m)
mash	puré (m) de patatas

pizza	pizza ff)
porridge	gachas (fpl)
omelette	tortilla (f) francesa
boiled	cocido en agua (adj)
smoked	ahumado (adj)
fried	frito (adj)
dried	seco (adj)
frozen	congelado (adj)
pickled	marinado (adj)
sweet	azucarado, dulce (adj)
salty	salado (adj)
cold	frío (adj)
hot	caliente (adj)
bitter	amargo (adj)
tasty	sabroso (adj)
to cook	cocer (vt) en agua
to cook	preparar (vt)
to fry	freír (vt)
to heat up	calentar (vt)
to salt	salar (vt)
to pepper	poner pimienta
to grate	rallar (vt)
peel	piel m
to peel	pelar (vt)
salt	sal (f)
salty	salado (adj)
to salt	salar (vt)
black pepper	pimienta (f) negra
red pepper	pimienta (f) roja
mustard	mostaza (f)
horseradish	rábano (m) picante
condiment	condimento (m)
spice	especia (f)
sauce	salsa (f)
vinegar	vinagre (m)
anise	anís (m)
basil	albahaca (f)
cloves	ClaVO (m)
ginger	jengibre (m)
coriander	Cilantro (m)

cinnamon	canela (f)
sesame	sésamo (m)
bay leaf	hoja (f) de laurel
paprika	paprika (f)
caraway	comino (m)
saffron	azafrán (m)

Words for eating / Condiciones de la comida

food	comida m
to eat	comer (vi, vt)
breakfast	desayuno (m)
to have breakfast	desayunar (vi)
lunch	almuerzo (m)
to have lunch	almorzar (vi)
dinner	cena (f)
to have dinner	cenar (vi)
appetite	apetito (m)
Enjoy your meal!	¡Que aproveche!
to open	abrir (vt)
to spill	derramar (vt)
to spill out	derramarse (vr)
to boil	hervir (vi)
to boil	hervir (vt)
boiled	hervido (adj)
to cool	enfriar (vt)
to cool down	enfriarse (vr)
taste, flavour	sabor (m)
aftertaste	regusto (m)
to be on a diet	adelgazar (vi)
diet	dieta (f)
vitamin	vitamina (f)
calorie	caloría ??
vegetarian	vegetariano (m)
vegetarian	vegetariano (adj)
fats	grasas (fpl)
proteins	proteínas (tpi)
carbohydrates	carbohidratos (mpl)
slice	loncha (f)
piece	pedazo (m)

crumb	miga (f)
spoon	cuchara (f)
knife	cuchillo (m)
fork	tenedor (m)
cup	taza (f)
plate	plato (m)
saucer	platillo (m)
serviette	servilleta ??
toothpick	mondadientes (m)

Restaurant — Restaurante

restaurant	restaurante (m)
coffee bar	cafetería ??
pub	bar (m)
tearoom	salón (m) de té
waiter	camarero (m)
waitress	camarera (f)
barman	barman (m)
menu	carta ??, menú (m)
wine list	carta ?? de vinos
to book a table	reservar una mesa
course, dish	plato (m)
to order	pedir (vt)
to make an order	hacer el pedido
aperitif	aperitivo (m)
starter	entremés (m)
dessert	postre (m)
bill	cuenta (f)
to pay the bill	pagar la cuenta
to give change	dar la vuelta
tip	propina (f)

Questionnaire — Cuestionario

name, first name	nombre (m)
family name	apellido (m)
date of birth	fecha (f) de nacimiento
place of birth	lugar (m) de nacimiento
nationality	nacionalidad (f)
place of residence	domicilio (m)
country	país (m)

profession	profesión (f)
gender, sex	sexo (m)
height	estatura (f)
weight	peso (m)

Relatives — parientes

mother	madre (f)
father	padre (m)
son	hijo (m)
daughter	hija (f)
younger daughter	hija (f) menor
younger son	hijo (m) menor
eldest daughter	hija (f) mayor
eldest son	hijo (m) mayor
brother	hermano (m)
sister	hermana (f)
cousin	primo (m)
cousin	prima (f)
mummy	mamá (f)
dad, daddy	papá (m)
parents	padres (mpl)
child	niño -a (m, f)
children	niños (mpl)
grandmother	abuela (f)
grandfather	abuelo (m)
grandson	nieto (m)
granddaughter	nieta (f)
grandchildren	nietos (mpl)
uncle	tío (m)
aunt	tía (f)
nephew	sobrino (m)
niece	sobrina (f)
mother-in-law	suegra (f)
father-in-law	suegro (m)
son-in-law	yerno (m)
stepmother	madrastra (f)
stepfather	padrastro (m)
infant	niño (m) de pecho
baby	bebé (m)

little boy	chico (m)
wife	mujer (f)
husband	marido (m)
married	esposo (m) , casado(m(
married	esposa (f) , casada(f) !!!
single	soltero (adj)
bachelor	soltero (m)
divorced	divorciado (adj)
widow	viuda (f)
widower	viudo (m)
relative	pariente (m)
close relative	pariente (m) cercano
distant relative	pariente (m) lejano
relatives	parientes (mpl)
orphan	huérfano (m) , huérfana (f)
guardian	tutor (m)
to adopt	ahijar (vt)
to adopt	ahijar (vt)

Friends and Collegues — Amigos y colegas

friend	amigo (m)
friend, girlfriend	amiga (f)
friendship	amistad (f)
to be friends	ser amigo
pal	amigóte (m)
pal	amigúete (f)
partner	compañero (m)
chief	jefe (m)
boss, superior	superior (m)
subordinate	subordinado (m)
colleague	colega (m, f)
acquaintance	conocido (m)
fellow traveller	compañero (m) de viaje
classmate	condiscípulo (m)
neighbour	vecino (m)
neighbour	vecina (f)
neighbours	vecinos(mpl)

Words about people — Palabras sobre personas

woman	mujer (f)
girl, young woman	muchacha (f)
bride, fiancee	novia (f)
beautiful	guapa (adj)
tall	alta (adj)
slender	esbelta (adj)
short	de estatura mediana
blonde	rubia (f)
brunette	morena (f)
ladies'	de señora (adj)
virgin	virgen (fj
pregnant	embarazada (adj)
man	hombre (m)
blond haired man	rubio (m)
dark haired man	moreno (m)
tall	alto (adj)
short	de estatura mediana
rude	grosero (adj)
stocky	rechoncho (adj)
robust	robusto (adj)
strong	fuerte (adj)
strength	fuerza (f)
stout, fat	gordo (adj)
swarthy	moreno (adj)
well-built	esbelto (adj)
elegant	elegante (adj)

Age — años

age	edad (f)
youth	juventud (f)
young	joven
younger	menor (adj)
older	mayor (adj)
young man	joven (m)
guy, fellow	adolescente (m), muchacho (m)
old man	anciano (m)

old woman	anciana (f)
adult	adulto
middle-aged	de edad media (adj)
elderly	de edad, anciano (adj)
old	viejo (adj)
to retire	jubilarse (vr)
pensioner	jubilado (m)

Children — niñas

child	niño -a (m,f)
children	niños (mpl)
twins	gemelos (mpl)
cradle	cuna (f)
rattle	sonajero (m)
nappy	pañal (m)
dummy, comforter	chupete (m)
pram	cochecito (m)
nursery	jardín (m) de infancia
babysitter	niñera m
childhood	infancia (f)
doll	muñeca (f)
toy	juguete (m)
construction set	mecano (m)
well-bred	bien criado (adj)
ill-bred	malcriado (adj)
spoilt	mimado (adj)
to be naughty	hacer travesuras
mischievous	travieso (adj)
mischievousness	travesura (f)
mischievous child	travieso (m)
obedient	obediente (adj)
disobedient	desobediente (adj)
docile	dócil (adj)
clever	inteligente (adj)
child prodigy	niño (m) prodigio
to kiss	besar
to kiss	besarse
family	familia (f)
family	familiar (adj)

couple	pareja (f)
marriage	matrimonio (m)
hearth	hogar (m) familiar
dynasty	dinastía m
date	cita (f)
kiss	beso (m)
love	amor (m)
to love	querer (vt)
beloved	querido (adj)
tenderness	ternura (f)
tender	tierno (adj)
faithfulness	fidelidad (f)
faithful	fiel (adj)
newlyweds	recién casados (pi)
honeymoon	luna (f) de miel
to get married	estar casada
to get married	casarse (vr)
wedding	boda (f)
golden wedding	bodas(fpl) de oro
anniversary	aniversario (m)
lover	amante (m)
mistress	amante (f)
adultery	adulterio (m)
to commit adultery	cometer adulterio
jealous	celoso (adj)
to be jealous	tener celos
divorce	divorcio (m)
to divorce	divorciarse (vr)
to quarrel	reñir (vi)
to be reconciled	reconciliarse (vr)
together	juntos (adv)
sex	sexo (m)
happiness	felicidad (f)
happy	feliz (adj)
misfortune	desgracia (f)
unhappy	desgraciado (adj)

Feelings — Sentimientos

feeling	sentimiento (m)

feelings	sentimientos (mpl)
to feel	sentir (vt)
hunger	hambre n
to be hungry	tener hambre
thirst	sed (f)
to be thirsty	tener sed
sleepiness	somnolencia m
to feel sleepy	tener sueño
tiredness	cansancio (m)
tired	cansado (adj)
to get tired	estar cansado
mood	humor (m)
boredom	aburrimiento (m)
to be bored	aburrirse (vr)
seclusion	soledad m
to seclude oneself	aislarse (vr)
to worry	inquietar (vt)
to be worried	inquietarse (vr)
anxiety	inquietud (f) , preocupación (f)
preoccupied	preocupado (adj)
to be nervous	estar nervioso
to panic	darse al pánico
hope	esperanza (f)
to hope	esperar (vi)
certainty	seguridad (f)
certain, sure	seguro (adj)
uncertainty	inseguridad (f)
uncertain	inseguro (adj)
drunk	borracho (adj)
sober	sobrio (adj)
weak	débil (adj)
happy	feliz (adj)
to scare	asustar (vt)
rage	furia (f) , rabia (f)
depression	depresión (f)
discomfort	incomodidad (f)
comfort	comodidad (f)
to regret	arrepentirse (vr)
regret	arrepentimiento (mj
bad luck	mala suerte (f)

sadness	tristeza (f)
shame	vergüenza (f)
merriment	júbilo (m)
enthusiasm	entusiasmo (m)
enthusiast	entusiasta (m)
to show enthusiasm	mostrar entusiasmo

Personal Traits — Rasgos personales

character	carácter (mj
character flaw	defecto (m)
mind	mente (f)
reason	razón (f)
conscience	consciencia (f)
habit	hábito (m)
ability	habilidad (f¡
can	poder (vt)
patient	paciente (adj)
impatient	impaciente (adj)
curious	curioso (adj)
curiosity	curiosidad (f)
modesty	modestia(f)
modest	modesto (adj)
immodest	inmodesto (adj)
lazy	perezoso (adj)
lazy person	perezoso (m)
cunning	astucia (f)
cunning	astuto (adj)
distrust	desconfianza (f)
distrustful	desconfiado (adj)
generosity	generosidad (f)
generous	generoso (adj)
talented	talentoso (adj)
talent	talento (m)
courageous	valiente (adj)
courage	coraje (m)
honest	honesto (adj)
honesty	honestidad (f)
careful	prudente (adj)
courageous	valeroso (adj)

serious	serio (adj)
strict	severo (adj)
decisive	decidido (adj)
indecisive	indeciso (adj)
shy, timid	tímido (adj)
shyness, timidity	timidez (f)
confidence	confianza (f)
to believe	creer (vt)
trusting, naive	confiado (adj)
sincerely	sinceramente (adv)
sincere	sincero (adj)
sincerity	sinceridad (f)
calm	calmado (adj)
frank	franco (adj) , abierto (adj)
naive, naive	ingenuo (adj)
absent-minded	distraído (adj)
funny	gracioso (adj)
greed	avaricia (f)
greedy	avaro (adj)
evil	tacaño (adj) , malvado (adj)
stubborn	terco (adj)
unpleasant	desagradable (adj)
selfish person	egoísta (m)
selfish	egoísta (adj)
coward	cobarde (m)
cowardly	cobarde (adj)

Sleep — El Sueño

to sleep	dormir (vi)
sleep, sleeping	sueño (m)
dream	sueño (m)
to dream	soñar (vi)
sleepy	adormilado (adj)
bed	cama (f)
mattress	colchón (m)
blanket	manta (f)
pillow	almohada m
sheet	sábana ?
insomnia	insomnio (m)

sleepless	de insomnio (adj)
sleeping pill	somnífero (m)
to take a sleeping pill	tomar el somnífero
to feel sleepy	tener sueño
to yawn	bostezar (vi)
to go to bed	irse a la cama
to make up the bed	hacer la cama
to fall asleep	dormirse (vr)
nightmare	pesadilla (f)
snoring	ronquido (m)
to snore	roncar (vi)
alarm clock	despertador (m)
to wake	despertar (vt)
to wake up	despertarse (vr)
to get up	levantarse (vr)
to wash oneself	lavarse (vr)

Laugh — Una Risa

humour	humor (m)
sense of humour	sentido (m) del humor
to have fun	divertirse (vr)
cheerful	alegre (adj)
merriment, fun	júbilo (m)
smile	sonrisa (f)
to smile	sonreír (vi)
to start laughing	echarse a reír
to laugh	reírse (vr)
laugh, laughter	risa (f)
anecdote	anécdota (f)
funny	gracioso (adj)
funny	ridículo (adj)
to joke, to be kidding	bromear (vi)
joke	broma (f)
joy	alegría (f)
to rejoice	alegrarse (vr)
glad	alegre (adj)

Communication — comunicación

communication	comunicación (f)

to communicate	comunicarse (vr)
conversation	conversación (f)
dialogue	diálogo (m)
discussion	discusión (f)
debate	debate (m)
to debate	debatir (vi)
interlocutor	interlocutor (m)
topic	tema (m)
point of view	punto (m) de vista
opinion	opinión (f)
speech	discurso (m)
discussion	discusión (f)
to discuss	discutir (vt)
talk	conversación (f)
to talk	conversar (vi)
meeting	reunión (f)
to meet	encontrarse (vr)
proverb	proverbio (m)
saying	dicho (m)
riddle	adivinanza (f)
to ask a riddle	contar una adivinanza
password	contraseña (f)
secret	secreto (m)
oath	juramento (m)
to swear	jurar (vt)
promise	promesa (f)
to promise	prometer (vt)
advice	Consejo (m)
to advise	aconsejar (vt)
to follow one's advice	escuchar (vt)
news	noticias (fpl)
sensation	sensación (f)
information	información (f)
conclusion	conclusión (f)
voice	voz (f)
compliment	cumplido (m)
kind	amable (adj)
word	palabra (f)
phrase	frase (f)
answer	respuesta (f)

truth	verdad (f)
lie	mentira (f)
thought	pensamiento (m)
idea	idea (f)
fantasy	fantasía (f)

Talk — Una Charla

respected	respetado (ac®
to respect	respetar (vt)
respect	respeto (m)
Dear...	Estimado ...
to introduce	presentar (vt)
to make acquaintance	presentarse???
intention	intención (f)
to intend	tener intención de ...
wish	deseo (m)
to wish	desear (vt)
surprise	sorpresa (f)
to surprise	sorprender (vt)
to be surprised	sorprenderse (vr)
to give	dar (vt)
to take	tomar (vt)
to give back	devolver (vt)
to return	retornar (vt)
to apologize	disculparse (vr)
apology	disculpa (f)
to forgive	perdonar (vt)
to talk	hablar (vi)
to listen	escuchar (vt)
to hear... out	escuchar hasta el final
to understand	comprender (vt)
to show	mostrar (vt)
to look at ...	mirar a ...
to call	llamar (vt)
to distract	molestar (vt)
to disturb	molestar (vt)
to pass	pasar (vt)
demand	petición (f)
to request	pedir (vt)

demand	exigencia (f)
to demand	exigir (vt)
to tease	motejar (vr)
to mock	burlarse (vr)
mockery, derision	burla (f)
nickname	apodo (m)
allusion	alusión (f)
to allude	aludir (vi)
to imply	sobrentender (vi)
description	descripción ?
to describe	describir (vt)
praise	elogio (m)
to praise	elogiar (vt)
disappointment	decepción ?
to disappoint	decepcionar (vt)
to be disappointed	estar decepcionado
supposition	suposición (f)
to suppose	suponer (vt)
warning, caution	advertencia ?
to warn	prevenir (vt)
to talk into	convencer (vt)
to calm down	calmar (vt)
silence	Silencio (m)
to keep silent	no decir nada
to whisper	susurrar (vt)
whisper	susurro (m)
frankly	francamente (adv)
in my opinion ...	en mi opinión ...
detail	detalle (m)
detailed	detallado (adj)
in detail	detalladamente (adv)
hint, clue	pista (f)
to give a hint	dar una pista
look	mirada (f)
to have a look	echar una mirada
fixed	fija (adj)
to blink	parpadear (vi)
to wink	guiñar un ojo
to nod	asentir con la cabeza
sigh	suspiro (m)

to sigh	suspirar (vi)
to shudder	estremecerse (vr)
gesture	gesto (m)
to touch	tocar (vt)
to seize	asir (vt)
to tap	palmear (vt)
Look out!	¡Cuidado!
Really?	¿De veras?
Good luck!	¡Suerte!
I see!	¡Ya veo!
It's a pity!	¡Es una lástima!

Agreement and Disagreement Acuerdo y desacuerdo

consent	acuerdo (m)
to agree	estar de acuerdo
approval	aprobación (f)
to approve	aprobar (vt)
refusal	rechazo (m)
to refuse	negarse (vr)
Great!	¡Excelente!
All right!	¡De acuerdo!
Okay!	¡Vale!
forbidden	prohibido (adj)
it's forbidden	está prohibido
incorrect	es imposible
to reject	incorrecto (adj)
to support	rechazar (vt)
to accept	apoyar (vt)
to confirm	aceptar (vt), confirmar (vt)
confirmation	confirmación (f)
permission	permiso (m)
to permit	permitir (vt)
decision	decisión (f)
to say nothing	no decir nada
condition	condición (f)
excuse	excusa (f)
praise	elogio (m)
to praise	elogiar (vt)

success	éxito (m)
successfully	con éxito (adv)
successful	exitoso (adj)
good luck	suerte (f)
Good luck!	¡Suerte!
lucky	de suerte (adj)
lucky	afortunado (adj)
failure	fiasco (m)
misfortune	infortunio (m)
bad luck	mala suerte (f)
unsuccessful	fracasado (adj)
catastrophe	catástrofe (f)
pride	orgullo (m)
proud	orgulloso (adj)
to be proud	estar orgulloso
winner	ganador (m)
to win	ganar (vi)
to lose	perder (vi)
try	tentativa (f)
to try	intentar (vt)
chance	chance (f)
shout	grito (m)
to shout	gritar (vi)
to start to cry out	comenzar a gritar
quarrel	riña (f)
to quarrel	reñir (vi)
fight	escándalo (m)
to have a fight	causar escándalo
conflict	conflicto (m)
misunderstanding	malentendido (m)
insult	insulto (m)
to insult	insultar (vt)
insulted	insultado (adj)
offence	ofensa (f)
to offend	ofender (vt)
to take offence	ofenderse (vr)
indignation	indignación (f)
to be indignant	indignarse (vr)
complaint	queja (f)
to complain	quejarse (vr)

apology	disculpa (f)
to apologize	disculparse (vr)
to beg pardon	pedir perdón
criticism	crítica (f)
to criticize	criticar (vt)
accusation	acusación (f)
to accuse	acusar (vt)
revenge	venganza(m)
to avenge	vengar (vt)
to pay back	pagar (vt)
disdain	desprecio (m)
to despise	despreciar (vt)
hatred, hate	odio (m)
to hate	odiar (vt)
nervous	nervioso (adj)
to be nervous	estar nervioso
angry	enfadado (adj)
to make angry	enfadar (vt)
to scold???	regañar (vt)
humiliation	humillación (f)
to humiliate	humillar (vt)
to humiliate oneself	humillarse (vr)
shock	choque (m)
to shock	chocar (vi)
trouble	molestia (f)
unpleasant	desagradable (adj)
fear	miedo (m)
terrible	terrible (adj)
scary	de miedo (adj)
horror	horror (m)
awful	horrible (adj)
to begin to tremble	empezar a temblar
to cry	llorar (vi)
to start crying	comenzar a llorar
tear	lágrima (f)
fault	culpa (f)
guilt	remordimiento (m)
dishonour	deshonra (f)
protest	protesta (f)
stress	estrés (m)

to disturb	molestar (vt)
to be furious	estar furioso
angry	enfadado (adj)
to end	terminar (vt)
to be scared	asustarse (vr)
to hit	golpear (vt)
to fight	pelear (vi)
to settle	regular (vt)
discontented	descontento (adj)
furious	furioso (adj)
It's not good!	¡No está bien!
It's bad!	¡Está mal!
Medicine	Medicina
Illness	Enfermedad
illness	enfermedad (f)
to be ill	estar enfermo
health	salud (f)
runny nose	resfriado (m)
tonsillitis	angina (f)
cold	resfriado (m)
to catch a cold	resfriarse (vr)
bronchitis	bronquitis (f)
pneumonia	pulmonía (f)
flu	gripe (f)
short-sighted	miope (adj)
long-sighted	présbita (adj)
squint	estrabismo (m)
squint-eyed	estrábico (m) (adj)
cataract	catarata (f)
glaucoma	glaucoma (f)
stroke	insulto (m)
heart attack	ataque (m) cardiaco
myocardial infarction	infarto (m) de miocardio
paralysis	parálisis (f)
to paralyse	paralizar (vt)
allergy	alergia (f)
asthma	asma (f)
diabetes	diabetes (m)
toothache	dolor (m) de muelas
caries	caries (f)

diarrhoea	diarrea (f)
constipation	estreñimiento (m)
stomach upset	molestia (f) estomacal
food poisoning	envenenamiento (m)
to poison oneself	envenenarse (vr)
arthritis	artritis (f)
rickets	raquitismo (m)
rheumatism	reumatismo (m)
atherosclerosis	ateroesclerosis (f)
gastritis	gastritis (f)
appendicitis	apendicitis (m)
cholecystitis	colecistitis (m)
ulcer	úlcera (f)
measles	sarampión (m)
German measles	rubéola (f)
jaundice	ictericia (f)
hepatitis	hepatitis (f)
schizophrenia	esquizofrenia (f)
rabies	rabia (f)
neurosis	neurosis (f)
concussion	conmoción (m) cerebral
cancer	cáncer (m)
sclerosis	esclerosis (f)
multiple sclerosis	esclerosis (f) múltiple
alcoholism	alcoholismo (m)
alcoholic	alcohólico (m)
syphilis	sífilis (f)
AIDS	SIDA (f)
tumour	tumor (m)
fever	fiebre (f)
malaria	malaria (f)
gangrene	gangrena (f)
seasickness	mareo (m)
epilepsy	epilepsia (f)
epidemic	epidemia (f)
typhus	tifus (m)
tuberculosis	tuberculosis (f)
cholera	cólera (f)
plague	peste (f)
Symptoms and Treatment	Síntomas y tratamiento.

symptom	síntoma (m)
temperature	temperatura m
fever	fiebre (f)
pulse	pulso (m)
giddiness	mareo (m)
hot	caliente (adj)
shivering	escalofrío (m)
pale	pálido (adj)
cough	tos (f)
to cough	toser (vi)
to sneeze	estornudar (vi)
faint	desmayo (?)
to faint	desmayarse (vr)
bruise	moradura (?)
bump	chichón (m)
to bruise oneself	golpearse (vr)
bruise	magulladura (f)
to get bruised	magullarse (vr)
to limp	cojear (vi)
dislocation	dislocación (f)
to dislocate	dislocar (vt)
fracture	fractura (f)
to have a fracture	tener una fractura
cut	corte (m)
to cut oneself	cortarse (vr)
bleeding	hemorragia (f)
burn	quemadura (f)
to burn oneself	quemarse (vr)
to prickle	pincharse (vr)
to prickle oneself	pincharse (vr)
to injure	herir (vt)
injury	herida m
wound	lesión (f)
trauma	trauma (m)
to be delirious	delirar (vi)
to stutter	tartamudear (vi)
sunstroke	insolación (f)
pain	dolor (m)
splinter	astilla (f)
sweat	sudor (m)

to sweat	sudar (vi)
vomiting	vómito (m)
convulsions	convulsiones (f)
pregnant	embarazada (adj)
to be born	nacer (vi)
delivery, labour	parto (m)
to labour	dar a luz
abortion	aborto (m)
respiration	respiración m
inhalation	inspiración (f)
exhalation	espiración ¡n
to breathe out	espirar (vi)
to breathe in	inspirar (vi)
disabled person	inválido (m)
cripple	mutilado (m)
drug addict	drogadicto (m)
deaf	sordo (adj)
dumb	mudo (adj)
deaf-and-dumb	sordomudo (adj)
mad, insane	loco (adj)
madman	loco (m)
madwoman	loca (f)
to go insane	volverse loco
gene	gen (m)
immunity	inmunidad m
hereditary	hereditario (adj)
congenital	de nacimiento (adj)
virus	virus (m)
microbe	microbio (m)
bacterium	bacteria (tj
infection	infección (f)
hospital	hospital (m)
patient	paciente (m)
diagnosis	diagnosis (f)
cure	cura (f)
treatment	tratamiento (m)
to get treatment	curarse (vr)
to treat	tratar (vt)
to nurse	cuidar (vt)
care	cuidados (mpl)

operation, surgery	operación m
to bandage	vendar (vt)
bandaging	vendaje (m)
vaccination	vacunación (f)
to vaccinate	vacunar (vt)
injection, shot	inyección (f)
to give an injection	aplicar una inyección
attack	asimiento(m)???
amputation	amputación (f)
to amputate	amputar (vt)
coma	??ma (f)
to be in a coma	estar en coma
intensive care	revitalización (f)
to recover	recuperarse (vr)
state	estado (m)
consciousness	consciencia (f)
memory	memoria (f)
to extract	extraer (vt)
filling	empaste (m)
to fill	empastar (vt)
hypnosis	hipnosis (f)
to hypnotize	hipnotizar (vt)
Medical specialties	Especialidades médicas
doctor	médico (m)
nurse	enfermera m
private physician	médico (m) personal
dentist	dentista (m)
ophthalmologist	oftalmólogo (m)
general practitioner	internista (m)
surgeon	cirujano (m)
psychiatrist	psiquiatra (m)
paediatrician	pediatra (m)
psychologist	psicólogo (m)
gynaecologist	ginecólogo (m)
cardiologist	cardiólogo (m)
Medicines	Medicinas
medicine, drug	medicamento (m), droga (f)
remedy	remedio (m)
to prescribe	prescribir
prescription	receta m

tablet, pill	tableta (f)
ointment	ungüento (m)
ampoule	ampolla (f)
mixture	mixtura (f), mezcla (f)
syrup	sirope (m)
pill	píldora (f)
powder	polvo (m)
bandage	venda m
cotton wool	algodón (m)
iodine	yodo (m)
plaster	tirita (f), curita (f)
eyedropper	pipeta (f)
thermometer	termómetro (m)
syringe	jeringa m
wheelchair	silla (f) de ruedas
crutches	muletas (fpl)
painkiller	anestésico (m)
laxative	purgante (m)
spirit, ethanol	alcohol (m)
medicinal herbs	hierba (f) medicinal
herbal	de hierbas (adj)
Smoking	De fumar
tobacco	tabaco (m)
cigarette	cigarrillo (m)
cigar	cigarro (m)
pipe	pipa (f)
packet	paquete (m)
matches	cerillas (fpl)
matchbox	caja (f) de cerillas
lighter	encendedor (m)
ashtray	cenicero (m)
cigarette case	pitillera (f)
cigarette holder	boquilla (f)
filter	filtro (m)
to smoke	fumar (vi, vt)
to light a cigarette	encender un cigarrillo
smoking	fumar(m)
smoker	fumador (m)
cigarette end	colilla (f)
smoke	humo (m)

ash ceniza (f)

Made in the USA
Las Vegas, NV
26 March 2024

87749454R10039